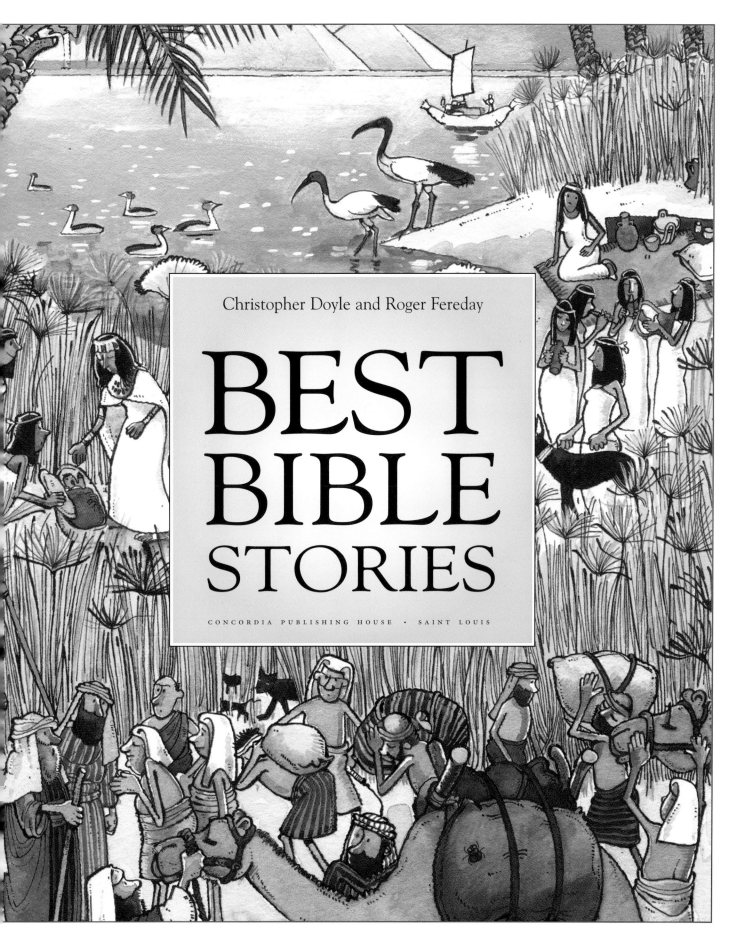

Christopher Doyle and Roger Fereday

BEST BIBLE STORIES

CONCORDIA PUBLISHING HOUSE • SAINT LOUIS

Contents

The Old Testament

The New Testament

The Old Testament

Beginnings, a rainbow, brothers who didn't get along, a baby in a basket, fierce battles, fires, some gentle beasts, and an adventure on a boat—these are just some of the things the Old Testament tells about.

God has always been there to save His people with His powerful actions. He wanted to watch over them and help them understand how much He loves them. But, as you'll see, the people didn't always want to listen.

Turn the page and read some of the Old Testament's best Bible stories!

In the beginning

I've got to find a way to stop that anteater from digging up the lettuce," said Adam.

There were also problems with the rhino trampling the

cucumbers and the monkeys picking the oranges. But generally, every creature lived happily with all the others. It was a beautiful, peaceful place God had created.

Of course it wasn't like that when He started. In the beginning there was just … well … darkness and emptiness.

First of all God made light so He could see what He was doing. He separated the light from the dark and called one of them day and the other one night.

Next He separated the earth from the sky. On the third day, He swished the water into one place and moved the dry areas in another to make the sea and land. While He was at it, He made every kind of plants, trees, and grasses.

Many of them grew fruit that was good to eat and they all produced seeds that made them grow widely over the earth.

He thought it would be a good idea to bring order to the lights in the sky, so He made the strong sun bring light for the day and silvery moon and the stars for the night sky. God was pleased with the way things were coming along.

After that, God made the sea creatures, millions of them, all different sorts, and then the birds to fly about. There were varied designs—long and short legged, brightly colored and dull, and lots of different types of beaks and feet. He made them to lay eggs to multiply and spread.

Next He made animals for the earth, from the smallest mouse to the largest elephant and everything in between. He made sure they could pair off and make many more, each of their own kind.

Last God made Adam and Eve, people in His own image. God made them to look after everything He had created, to tend the garden and be in charge of all the animals. He told His new people they could eat the fruit from any of the trees and plants in the garden … except for one special tree, the tree that bore the fruit of the knowledge of good and evil. They had to leave that one alone.

God knew that what He had done was very good, so He rested.

God made everything to live in harmony and everything work well together. But, sadly, the harmony didn't last. The Evil One came in the form of a serpent. He tempted the people by lying to them. They disobeyed God.

This made God sad and angry. Although He punished His people, God promised to make things right again. God promised that one day He would send a Savior to His people.

The great flood

After a while, God looked at the world He had made and saw how wicked and evil the people had become. The only man He was pleased with was Noah.

"Noah," said God, "I am sad when I see what's happening in the world. I have decided to destroy it."

"Everything and everybody?" asked Noah, feeling rather worried.

"I will send a great flood," said God. "Only you and your family will be saved. You're a faithful man and I have a plan I want you to carry out." Then God told Noah, in great detail, what to do.

When Noah arrived home, he told his family "I have to build a huge boat, an ark. It must be 133 meters long and 22 meters wide and 13 meters high. It's got to have three decks and a roof and, and …"

"Hold on a minute," said his wife. "This is a big job. How are you going to do it?"

Noah explained that their sons, Shem, Ham and Japheth, and their wives, would all lend a hand. There was another part to God's plan.

"God said to collect the male and female of every animal, bird, and insect and take them in the ark too," added Noah.

Noah and his family worked hard and soon everything was ready.

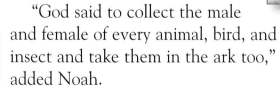

Noah hurried his family and all the animals into the ark as the first drops of rain darkened the dust on the ground. God shut the door behind them and for forty days and nights the rain came down in torrents. As the water level rose, the ark floated higher. Everyone else and all the other creatures drowned in the flood.

Then one day the rain stopped. A breeze danced across the waves and the water gradually started to dry up. There was a scraping noise, then a bump, and the ark came to rest on the top of Mount Ararat.

Noah sent a raven out but it just flew around. He sent out a dove but it soon came back. A week later, Noah sent the dove out again and it returned carrying a twig from an olive tree.

"The water must be going down!" he cried. Another week later he sent the dove out again, and this time it did not return.

Finally God told Noah to open the door and the animals crept, crawled, trotted, and flew out of the ark. Noah praised God.

"I promise never to do this again," said God. "As a sign, I shall put My rainbow in the heavens."

As Noah and his family watched, the sun's rays streaked over the horizon and a beautiful rainbow spread across the sky. It was a sign of God's faithfulness to His people.

Sharing the land

"Hey! Come on, move your sheep off my pasture," called one of Lot's shepherds, poking a ram in the side with his staff.

"Don't you start that," said the other man. "Leave my sheep alone. I was here first. Go find your own patch of grass."

And so went the arguments. The trouble was that Lot and Abram had become very rich as they traveled around Canaan and during the time they spent in Egypt. Now they were back in Canaan and each owned huge flocks of sheep, goats, and cattle, as well as large amounts of gold and silver.

"We've journeyed around Canaan long enough," said Abram. "We shall stay here, between Bethel and Ai, for a while."

The tented village was a busy place with all manner of activities going on. Wherever you looked, there were people grinding grain, preparing food, or weaving cloth. Chickens and goats roamed freely between the tents and sometimes got in the way.

"But Uncle Abram," said Lot, "between us we have too many animals for this pasture to support. The men are arguing all the time and things could turn nasty."

"This can't go on," said Abram. "We are relatives; your men and my men shouldn't be quarreling. The time has come for us to separate."

Abram told Lot he could choose whichever part of the land he wanted. Once that was done, Lot could go one way and Abram would go the other. This was a generous offer as he gave Lot first pick. Lot considered carefully.

"It looks to me that the Jordan Valley has plenty of water," said Lot. "It's fertile, like the land of Egypt and like the stories I've heard about the Garden of Eden. That's where I'll go."

So Lot set off to the east and settled his side of the family amongst the cities in the valley. Abram stayed in the land of Canaan.

After Lot left, God spoke to Abram. "Abram, look around you in every direction. All the land you can see I will give to you and your descendants forever. Your family will grow so large you won't be able to count them all."

Faithful Abram believed everything God said. So he moved camp and settled near Hebron where he built an altar to praise God and to remember what He had told him.

Quarreling brothers!

I'm starving! Give me some of that lentil stew."

The large, hairy form of Esau filled the entrance to the tent. He had been out hunting and was sweaty and smelly.

"Oh, please! You're not coming in here like that, are you?" said Jacob, his twin brother. "Aren't you going to wash first?"

Jacob was altogether more sensitive and preferred to spend his time at home. But there was something else that annoyed Jacob.

Esau had been born first, so he was the older brother. That meant he would be given their father's blessing and would inherit everything when their father, Isaac, died. Jacob wanted it all for himself and he had a plan.

"Will you sell me father's blessing for some delicious food?" said Jacob.

"You can have it. Just give me the food." And so Jacob tricked Esau out of his inheritance.

Many years passed. Isaac, their father, was now old and blind. He called Esau into his tent.

"Esau, I haven't long to live. Before I give you my blessing, go and hunt some game and prepare me some savory meat, just the way I like it."

Esau set off to go hunting, but Rebekah, the boys' mother, had overheard. Jacob was her favorite son and she devised a plan to trick Isaac.

"Jacob," she said, "go and fetch two young goats and I'll prepare a meal for your father. You dress up in Esau's best clothes and get ready to take it in."

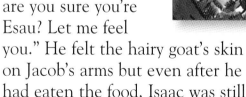

"Who's that coming in to my tent?" asked Isaac.

"It's me, Esau," Jacob lied.

"Mmmm! That food smells delicious. But are you sure you're Esau? Let me feel you." He felt the hairy goat's skin on Jacob's arms but even after he had eaten the food, Isaac was still not certain.

"Come here and kiss me, my son," he said. As Jacob leaned near, Isaac could smell Esau's clothes and believed this was his elder son. So Isaac blessed him and promised that he would inherit everything. The trick worked!

When Esau returned, he prepared a meal for his father.

"Here you are, father, your favorite meal," said Esau. "Now will you give me your blessing?"

Isaac was confused.

"Who was I talking to just now?" asked Isaac, growing angry. "It looks like your brother has tricked me into giving him the blessing!"

Esau was furious!

"That's the second time he's tricked me. I'll kill him!"

Jacob was frightened and ran away. He went to his uncle Laban's house, where he stayed for 20 years.

"But he'll know it's me," said Jacob. "Esau has hairy arms and smells horrible!"

"We'll put the goat's skin on you. He'll never tell the difference." So Jacob took the food in.

Jacob and Esau didn't remain enemies forever. They met again years later. God had blessed them both and helped them to make peace with each other.

Sold to be a slave

"Look who's coming," said one of the brothers. "Joseph, the dreamer, who thinks we're all to bow down to him."

"Bow to Joseph! Not me," said another. "I've had enough of his dreams. Let's get rid of him once and for all."

"Yeah!" said a third. "We'll slit his throat and say a wild animal killed him."

As you can see, they didn't like their younger brother. Joseph was their father's favorite and Jacob had given the boy a special robe. It was long, had big sleeves and lots of colors. No wonder his brothers were jealous of him.

"Look," said Reuben, "let's not be too hasty. Let's just put him into one of these old wells and leave him there." Reuben planned to rescue Joseph later.

"Well, since he is our brother we could do that," the others said.

So, the moment Joseph arrived, they grabbed him, took off the fancy robe, and threw him into the dry well. Then, as calm as you like, they sat down to finish their lunch.

While they were eating, the brothers saw an Ishmaelite camel train passing by. The animals were heavily loaded and were being taken to Egypt. One of the brothers had an idea.

"Let's sell Joseph to these traders and make a bit of money on him," said Judah.

The brothers pulled Joseph out of the well and sold him as a slave for twenty shekels of silver. The traders tied their new slave to a camel and set off again.

Reuben had been away while this happened. When he returned, he looked in the well

and was very upset to find Joseph gone. He cried and tore his clothes.

"What's the problem, Reuben?"

"Joseph is gone! What am I going to do?" cried Reuben.

They devised a plan. One of them killed a goat and they dipped the fancy robe in the blood. When they returned home, they went to see their father.

"Oh, father, on our way home we found this," one of them lied. "Do you think it looks a bit like Joseph's robe?"

Jacob was convinced a wild animal had torn his favorite son to pieces. He could not be consoled and vowed he would be broken-hearted until he died.

Meanwhile, many miles away, Joseph was sold to Potiphar, who was captain of the Egyptian king's palace guard. It was the start of many adventures Joseph had dreamed about. You see, God had given Joseph a special gift; it was the gift of understanding dreams about the future.

Joseph grew up to be a powerful man in Egypt. And he forgave his brothers for trying to hurt him.

This was all part of God's plan for Joseph. God has plans for us too. We can trust God to protect us. And we can forgive others who hurt us.

The baby in the river

"By order of Pharaoh, king of Egypt," shouted the messenger, "all Israelite baby boys are to be thrown into the River Nile."

You see, Pharaoh was worried. The numbers of the Israelites had grown and he was scared they might rebel or join enemy armies to fight Pharaoh and the Egyptians.

The king had already tried other ways to keep the Israelites down. He had ordered that they should work hard by making many bricks to supply the builders. He had forced them to do much more work in the fields. He put slave drivers over them to wear them down. He had still another trick up his sleeve.

"You midwives," he said, "when you're helping the Hebrew women give birth, make sure you kill any baby boys."

The midwives were afraid of God and they didn't obey the king. So the numbers of the Israelites had continued to increase. That's why the king was taking such drastic action.

One day, a woman from the Israelite tribe of Levi gave birth to a baby boy. Because she feared Pharaoh's command, she hid him for three months. When she could keep her secret no longer, she decided on a plan.

"I'll weave a basket," she said to her

daughter, "then cover it in tar to make it watertight. I'll put the baby inside and float him at the edge of the river. You stay hidden and keep watch."

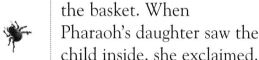

As the girl watched, Pharaoh's daughter came along. While she swam in the river, her

the basket. When Pharaoh's daughter saw the child inside, she exclaimed, "What a lovely baby boy! I will keep him as my own."

The baby's sister left her hiding place and bowed low.

"Your Highness, would you like me to find one of the Hebrew women to nurse the child for you?"

The princess agreed. It was the baby's own mother who bustled along to take back her son! The princess ordered her to look after the child and even paid her for doing so. When the boy grew up, he had to return to the palace and the princess adopted him as her own son. She named him "Moses."

When Moses grew into a man, he was faithful to God and became one of the most important Israelite leaders. His life shows how God watches over His people so He might deliver them from the slavery of sin.

servants walked along the bank with the towels. Suddenly the princess shrieked.

"There in the reeds," she cried. "Fetch it for me." Her maid waded in and picked up

The walls of Jericho

"So let me get this right," said one of the soldiers. "We will march around the city …"

"Once a day for six days," his friend added.

"Okay, once a day for six days. We carry our weapons but we don't use them."

"That's correct. We march in front of the priests with their trumpets. Behind them will be the Ark of the Covenant, which is the presence of God. Then there'll be a rear guard following."

"Well, that sounds easy," said the first soldier and he fell into rank.

Jericho had strong walls and there were many soldiers to defend it if it were attacked. And that was exactly the point. The Israelites were not conducting an ordinary war. This battle was to be fought God's way, following the instructions He gave them to march with the Ark.

Shortly before this, two spies from the Israelite camp had gone into the city to look around. They were almost discovered but had been hidden from the Jericho soldiers by a woman called Rahab. She helped them by using a rope to lower them down the city wall so they could escape. In return, the spies promised Rahab and her family would be safe during the battle. To remind them where she

march around the city seven times. As before, the seven priests will blow their trumpets and march before those who carry the Ark. When we complete the seventh time around, they will give a long blast on their horns. At that point all of you must give a great, loud shout. Then the city will be ours for the taking."

The Israelite army trusted in God and followed Joshua's orders. At the end of the seventh trip around the city, the priests blew loud and hard and the soldiers shouted. Suddenly cracks appeared in the thick city walls and they crumbled and fell! The Israelites ran into the city and destroyed everything and everyone— except for Rahab and her family. The soldiers had also been instructed to rescue items of valuable metal and these were all put in the treasury.

Joshua became famous in the

lived, Rahab had tied some red string to the window frame of her house.

On the seventh day, Joshua, the Israelites' leader, gave new orders.

"Today," said Joshua, "God says we

land as the news of his victory spread.

From that day on, Jericho stood as a reminder that God is always present with His people and protects His faithful followers.

Stronger than a lion

Awakened from his sleep, Samson was grabbed by a group of men—and he couldn't shake them off!

The Philistines were fed up with Samson. He had great strength; he had even wrestled and overcome a lion. Samson often used his strength against the Philistines. Once, armed with only the jaw bone of a donkey, he killed a thousand of them. To deal with Samson, the Philistines bribed Delilah to find out the secret of his strength. Samson, of course, didn't want to tell.

"Oh, Samson, you don't really love me," Delilah whined. "If you did, you would tell me."

"For goodness' sake!" growled Samson. "If you have to know, it's my hair. If it's cut, then my strength will vanish."

Samson then drifted off to sleep. Delilah called the Philistines and told them to fetch a barber. He came and shaved off Samson's hair! When the Philistines seized him this time, he couldn't get away.

"Gouge out his eyes," the leader ordered, "and take him away to Gaza."

Poor Samson, now blind, worked in the prison mill. But as time passed, his hair grew back.

The Philistines were holding a great feast for their god, Dagon. As people gathered for the party, someone decided to bring Samson out to make fun of him. They were glad he had been captured and couldn't cause any more trouble. They stood Samson between the great pillars that held up the building. After a while, people grew bored and went back to the party inside the house and on the rooftop gardens.

"Boy," whispered Samson to a child. "Put my hands on the pillars. Let me feel where they are."

He felt the smooth stone and flexed his muscles.

"Lord, give me strength this one last time and I shall die with these Philistines."

With that, Samson strained and pushed. There was a scraping noise and the stones shifted. The whole building shuddered and suddenly came crashing down in a shower of bricks and rubble. About 3,000 Philistines died as they were crushed by the falling building. God gave Samson strength and he had his revenge against the enemy.

God gives us strength against our enemies—sin, death, and the devil—in the person of Jesus.

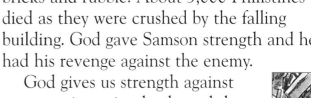

David the giant-killer

David had spent all day on the mountain-side looking after his father's sheep. After gathering the flock for the night, he went home.

"Ah, my son," said his father, Jesse. "I have a job for you. Go to your brothers at the battle front to see how they are."

The next day David set off with food and presents for his brothers. When he arrived, the soldiers were preparing to fight. David found his brothers and started chatting when a huge man appeared from the ranks of the Philistine army.

"It's Goliath from Gath," someone said. David listened to what Goliath had to say.

"I am the champion," bellowed Goliath. "You Israelites must choose one man to fight me. If he wins, we shall be your slaves. If I win, you shall be our slaves."

"It's been the same thing for forty days, morning and evening," said David's brother. "Everyone's scared of him. Look, he's nearly 10 feet tall. His armor is made of bronze and that spear is as thick as the beam from a weaver's loom."

"Who does this Philistine think he is?" asked David. "I'm not afraid of him."

When King Saul heard what David had said, he commanded the boy to be brought to him. David stepped forward boldly.

"If no one else will fight this giant, then I shall," he said.

"You are just a boy," replied Saul. "How can you fight Goliath, who has been a soldier since he was a boy?"

David told Saul about the times he had killed bears and lions when they threatened to attack the sheep.

"If God protected me against wild animals, then He'll protect me against this Philistine too."

"Go then, and may the Lord go with you," said Saul. He gave David his armor to wear but it was so big and

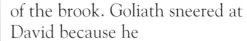

of the brook. Goliath sneered at David because he was so young and small.

"Come here, boy. I'll rip you apart and feed you to the birds!" shouted Goliath. Then he started to lumber forward. David fitted one of the stones into his sling, swung it around his head, and flung it at the giant. The stone landed and sank right in the center of Goliath's forehead. Goliath groaned and fell forward, dead.

David took Goliath's sword and cut off the giant's head. The Israelites cheered and charged forward. The Philistines, seeing their champion beaten, were so scared they ran away and the Israelite army chased them all the way back to Gath. The Israelites were victorious because David trusted God to help him.

David became a hero.

heavy he couldn't walk! David took off the armor and went out with just his stick and his sling. He went down to the brook and chose five smooth stones. Then the boy and giant stood opposite each other on either side

When he grew up, he became a great king. Many years later, one of David's descendants—Jesus—was born to be the King of kings and Lord of all.

The one true God

He's got to be joking!" said one of the onlookers. "A wet altar won't light."

Elijah had ordered water to be poured over the altar for the third time; everything was absolutely soaked.

God's people, the Israelites, had to be taught a lesson.

Ahab, the king, had worshiped the idol Baal instead of listening to God, so Elijah warned him there would be a drought. Ahab sent out messengers to try to find pasture for the animals while his wife, Jezebel, arranged for God's prophets to be killed. Only Elijah was left. When he came to see Ahab, the king was angry.

"So it's you," said the king, "the troublemaker of Israel."

"I haven't caused this trouble," replied Elijah. "You are the one who followed Baal. If you had obeyed God, things would be different. God will show you how powerful He is."

Then, the false prophets were called to Mount Carmel. Elijah told them to choose one of the two bulls he had brought.

"We shall each set up an altar and put the meat on it," explained Elijah. "But do not set fire to it. You must call Baal and I shall call on the Lord. Whichever sends down fire will show himself to be the one true God. You go first."

All 450 prophets of Baal called to their idol for hours, but nothing happened.

Elijah eventually called a halt. Then he rebuilt the altar of the Lord using 12 stones to represent the 12 tribes of Israel. Having prepared everything, he doused the whole thing in water.

"Lord, the one true God of Israel," prayed Elijah, "You know I have been faithful

to You all this time and have always done what You wanted me to. Show these people that You are their God."

God answered faithful Elijah's prayer. With a huge flash, flames came and burned the altar—meat, wood, stones, and all; and it dried up all the water.

The people were amazed.

"The Lord is God, no doubt about it!" they cried.

Elijah told them to round up the prophets of Baal, making sure none escaped. They were all killed.

Soon after that the drought broke and rain fell again on Israel.

God heard Elijah's prayers and answered them. God hears and answers our prayers in Jesus' name too.

Thrown to the lions

It's no good," moaned the king. "I won't sleep a wink tonight. Oh, what have I done?" King Darius had been tricked, you see, and now he was hoping against hope that Daniel would be safe.

Daniel was one of several Jewish noblemen who had been brought to Babylon many years before. They had proved themselves to be wise and earned good jobs in the court.

Kings came and went but Daniel was always well regarded. He was able to tell the meaning of the kings' dreams and as a reward was given a very important job. But other officers and officials of the court were jealous and tried to find a way to get rid of him.

Through it all, Daniel and the other Jews remained faithful to God.

Now Daniel, with two others, were put in charge of 120 governors in the kingdom. Darius was so impressed with Daniel that he considered putting him in charge of the whole country. This made the others even more jealous.

"Oh king, may you live forever," said the supervisors and governors (you had to start like that, otherwise the king could have you amputated right below the chin). "We have all agreed that you should issue a new decree.

We think you should say that for the next month, everyone should worship or pray to you only. Anyone who doesn't do this should be thrown to the lions."

The king rather liked the idea so he agreed. But Daniel and the other Jewish people knew there was only one God; they would worship only Him. The officials caught Daniel worshiping God as he always did, three times a day. "We've got him!" they cried triumphantly.

When they told King Darius about it, he had to punish Daniel as the law said. So Daniel was thown to the lions.

"I expect he's being torn limb from limb as I lie awake," whimpered the king that night. He was upset because he was rather fond of Daniel and didn't want to lose him.

When the sun rose the next morning, the king ran to the punishment block.

"Daniel!" he called through the door. "Are you all right? Did your God protect you? Please answer me if you can."

"Oh, I'm fine," called Daniel. "God protected me. These lions did not hurt me."

The king was so relieved he ordered the guards to bring Daniel out.

Because God had protected Daniel from the lions, King Darius worshiped Him too. God protects all those who believe and trust in Him.

Jonah runs away!

Jonah," said God. "As one of my prophets I want you to go to the city of Nineveh and tell the people how wicked they all are. Tell them they must mend their ways."

Jonah was afraid to go to Nineveh and couldn't face the thought of this task.

I'll run away so God can't find me, thought Jonah. In Joppa he found a ship bound for Tarshish, paid the captain his fare, and scurried off below decks.

The ship set sail, but it wasn't long before angry looking clouds billowed, the wind raged, and great waves lashed the ship. The crew, afraid the ship would sink, started calling out to their gods to save them. They threw the cargo over the sides to make the ship lighter. But none of this did any good. The captain went into the hold and found Jonah asleep.

"Wake up!" shouted the captain. Jonah came up on deck and found the sailors drawing straws to see who had caused the bad weather. Jonah drew the short straw!

"Tell us what you have done and why we are having such awful weather," they demanded. Jonah was very ashamed as he told how he was trying to hide from God.

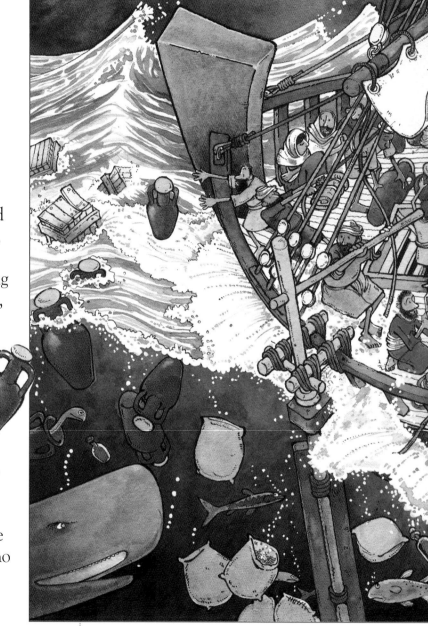

"You must throw me overboard, and then the sea will become calm again," said Jonah. So the sailors hurled him over the side into the sea. Instantly the weather calmed and they were safe.

But what about Jonah? God made a large fish swim by and swallow him up. Jonah slithered down the fish's throat and lay in the damp, smelly darkness of its stomach.

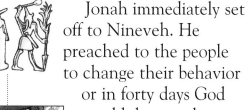

It took three days and nights for Jonah to learn his lesson, but eventually he said to God that he was sorry for disobeying Him. The fish swam near the shore and spat Jonah out.

Jonah immediately set off to Nineveh. He preached to the people to change their behavior or in forty days God would destroy them and their city.

The people listened to Jonah and they said sorry to God. So He decided not to destroy the city after all. This made Jonah angry.

"What right have you to be so cross?" God asked. Then Jonah went to sit on a hillside and sulked in the hot sun.

God made a plant grow up to give Jonah some shade. Jonah was very pleased about this. But the next day God made the plant wither and die. Jonah again suffered in the heat and he shouted at God.

"I might as well be dead," he moaned.

"Why are you so angry about the plant?" asked God. "You didn't make it grow but now you feel sorry for it! Shouldn't I, then, have pity on the thousands of people in Nineveh after they have repented?"

At last Jonah understood. God sent him to tell the people to repent. His message was about God's grace for all people. To accomplish this, God would send a Savior who would bring forgiveness, peace, and salvation to the world.

The New Testament

The beginning of the New Testament is about Jesus' life. Just as He promised in the Old Testament, God sent His own Son, Jesus, to live on earth and show how much God loves us. Jesus is true God, who bears the punishment for our sin and brings us forgiveness and salvation.

In the New Testament, we see how Jesus performed miracles, healed people, provided for all their needs, and rescued them from danger and forgave their sins. Finally we see that Jesus died, was buried, and was raised to life on Easter, in victory over sin, death, and the devil.

A very special delivery

"You can sleep in the stable at the back. There's plenty of hay and no one will disturb you." The innkeeper waved a hand and went back inside to see to his other customers.

The innkeeper's wife smiled as she brought them a small loaf and a few figs to eat. She knew her husband wouldn't turn this couple away like some others in town had.

"Everywhere is full because of this census," she said. "These Romans, they're always counting what they've got so they can write it in the emperor's record books."

That, of course, was why Joseph had brought Mary to Bethlehem. He was a descendant of David, so this was considered to be his home city and where he had to register himself and his wife in the census.

His wife, now that is an interesting story. You see, he'd had this dream.

"Don't be afraid to take Mary as your wife," the angel had said. "The baby she will have is going to be very special. Mary has been chosen to be the mother of God."

Joseph, a humble carpenter, did just as the angel had told him. Now they were in Bethlehem, tired, uncomfortable, and having to sleep with the animals. Then, as if that weren't enough, the baby was born that very night!

Meanwhile, on a hillside outside the city, there were some shepherds. They had

gathered their flocks for the night and were dozing near the dying embers of the fire. To them it seemed to be a night like any other.

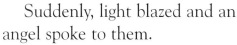

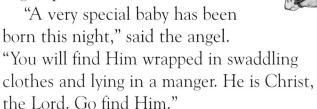

Suddenly, light blazed and an angel spoke to them.

"A very special baby has been born this night," said the angel. "You will find Him wrapped in swaddling clothes and lying in a manger. He is Christ, the Lord. Go find Him."

The shepherds were scared but they recognized that this was a very important event.

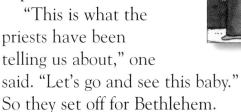

"This is what the priests have been telling us about," one said. "Let's go and see this baby." So they set off for Bethlehem.

When they arrived, they found Joseph looking very pleased and Mary looking worn out. Lying in the animals' hay box, just as the angel had said, was the baby, Jesus. The shepherds knelt and bowed their heads.

"How wonderful this is," they said in hushed voices. "Praise God for this special baby." Praise Him for sending us a Savior."

Then they went back to their sheep. Joseph was happy it was all over. But Mary thought about everything that had happened.

After all, through her, God had kept His promise to send the world a Savior!

A river baptism

"Well, I know he's been out in the desert for a while," said the woman as she squeezed the water out of her washing, "but eating locusts and wild honey is a bit strange."

"Who is he?" asked her friend as they knelt next to the river.

"His name is John.

He's Elizabeth and Zechariah's son. Some people say he's gone a bit wild."

Nevertheless, a great crowd had come from Jerusalem and Judea to hear what John had to say. Only a few days before, he had come to the river, shouting out in his loud, gruff voice.

"Prepare the way of the Lord and make a straight path for Him!" he bellowed. It certainly made people stop to listen. He had explained to the tax collectors to collect only what was due and no more. To the soldiers he had said they should be content with the wages they received and they should not rob people. He had a message for everyone: repent and be sorry for the things they had done wrong and live their life a better way. Then he baptized them in the river.

Among the crowd were some Pharisees and Sadducees, important people from the temple. They had come in their prayer shawls with their boxes of law strapped to their heads to look good in front of the crowd. John turned to them.

"You brood of vipers!" he shouted. "Do you think you will be saved just because you claim to be descendants of Abraham? The axe will be put to the root of the tree that does not bear good fruit."

The people understood that John was talking about the temple officials. They had not really meant to be sorry when they came to the river for baptism; it was all just for show.

Just then a man stepped out from the crowd. Jesus had come to see His cousin, John. He asked John to baptize Him. But John was embarrassed.

"I shouldn't baptize You; rather You should baptize me."

"It is proper to do it like this for now," said Jesus. "This is what God wants."

So, in front of that crowd, John took Jesus and lowered Him beneath the water as though washing away anything He might have done wrong.

As Jesus surfaced, a dove flew down and settled on Him. To the crowd's amazement, a voice from heaven said, "This is My Son. I am well pleased with Him."

God had spoken! The dove was a sign that the Holy Spirit was with Jesus. It marked the new beginning, the start of the work Jesus was to do on earth.

When we're baptized, the Holy Spirit comes in the water and the Word of God. Our sins are washed away once and for all.

Water, wine, and a wedding

Dear Jesus, you are invited to a wedding and reception at The Well House in Cana, Galilee. Usual arrangements – feasting all day. Please bring some friends if you like."

Jesus was happy to accept the invitation and He took His disciples with Him. It was certainly a good day for a wedding; clear skies and plenty of sunshine. The bride looked radiant and the groom looked very pleased with his new wife.

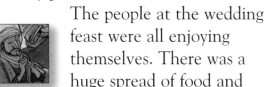

The people at the wedding feast were all enjoying themselves. There was a huge spread of food and some of the best wine for miles around.

But later, during the afternoon, the servants were looking very upset and fussing about near the cellar door. Jesus' mother, Mary, was also at the wedding. She spoke with the servants then hurried over to where Jesus was sitting.

"Jesus!" she said. "What do You think? The wine has run out. There is nothing left for the guests to drink."

"Why are you telling Me?" said Jesus. "It's not the right time for Me to do anything now."

Mary thought for a moment then, turning to the servants, she said, "Just do whatever He tells you."

There were six large stone jars in the yard.

They were normally used in washing rituals the Jews had to perform. Each held twenty to thirty gallons. Jesus told the servants to fill the jars with water. They did as Jesus said.

"Now," said Jesus, "dip out some of the water and take it to the chief steward in charge of the feast." The servants carried out His instructions just as Mary had told them to. The steward took the cup the servants offered and took a sip. His eyebrows shot up in surprise. Up until then, neither he nor the servants knew it but the water had turned into the best wine there was. The steward couldn't believe what he had tasted and had to take another drink to convince himself.

"Excuse me, sir, but might I have a word?" said the steward, tugging at the bridegroom's sleeve. "At other weddings, most people serve the best wine first. In this way, when they serve the poorer quality wine, the guests will already have drunk so much they won't notice. You, on the other hand, have saved the best wine until now."

Jesus' disciples saw what He had done. They knew He was someone very special to perform such a miracle.

It showed that Jesus is God's Son, and as true God, He has power over all things. To the people at the wedding, this showed that Jesus was the Messiah the Old Testament promised.

Bed-man walks!

Jesus had been traveling around the region and finally made His way back to Capernaum. When word got out that He was back, a great crowd came to see Him in the house where He was teaching. Even some Pharisees and teachers of the Law had come. People filled the streets and filled up the doorways.

"Pardon us, please. Make way there!" Along a side street, four men struggled to squeeze through. Between them they carried their friend who was paralyzed. He couldn't walk and had not moved off his bed for years, but they were sure Jesus would be able to heal him.

"Come on," one of them said, "we are nearly there." They rounded the corner and found the house. But they saw there was no way they were going to get in.

"Just look at the crowds!" another exclaimed. "How are we going to get our friend, on his bed, into that house?"

It certainly seemed a problem. As they stood, one of them noticed the stairs leading up the side of the house.

"Come here, I've got an idea," he said. As they struggled up the steps, the owner of the house followed them. He reached the top and found the men tearing away the roof.

"Lend us some rope," called one of the men. The house owner was so amazed that he gave them

the rope and watched in silence.

Everyone in the house looked up as the paralyzed man, still on his bed, was lowered through the hole, right into the space in front of Jesus! When Jesus saw how much the men trusted Him for help, He turned to the man on the bed.

"My friend, your sins are forgiven," said Jesus. There was a gasp from the Pharisees who were there, each with a little box of the law strapped to their head.

"How can this man say that?" they muttered. "Surely only God can forgive sins!" Jesus was aware of what they were saying and looked at them.

"Why are you muttering?" said Jesus. "What is easier to say, 'Your sins are forgiven,' or, 'Stand up and walk'?" He didn't wait for an answer. "Well, I'll do this so you'll know that I have the authority on earth to forgive sins."

Turning to the paralyzed man, He said, "Stand up, friend. Pick up your bed and go home."

The man sat up, wiggled his toes, then stood. He picked up the bed he had been lying on all those years and carried it out of the room, smiling and thanking God.

"Well, I've never seen anything like that," somebody said. Others cheered and cried out, "How marvelous! What amazing things we've seen today!"

Jesus, who is God the Son, forgave the man and healed him. Jesus forgives us, too, and heals our lives from the sickness of sin.

Jesus stills a storm

What a day it had been! In the hot sunshine, Jesus had talked all afternoon to the crowds who had followed Him to the shore of Lake Galilee. There were so many people that Jesus had climbed into a boat before the crowd pushed Him into the water. He had told parables and stories and taught about His Father's kingdom. Now the evening had arrived and it was beginning to cool down.

"Let's go across to the other side of the lake," said Jesus. So some of His disciples hauled on the ropes to pull up the sails and pushed off from the shore.

Jesus was so tired, He snuggled down on a pillow in the stern and drifted off to sleep. Before long, though, clouds gathered and a strong wind blew up. Waves crashed about on the lake. Water slopped over the sides and threatened to swamp the boat. While some of the disciples tried to take down the sails, others

took to the oars to try to row to shore. Some made an effort to bail out the water but others were so scared they didn't know what to do.

"Master, Master, wake up!" the disciples cried. "We're all going to drown if this weather carries on."

Jesus opened His eyes and sat up. He seemed to be unaware of any danger.

"Why are you frightened? Where is your faith?" He asked. Jesus stood in the boat as it pitched and rolled. He held up His hand and spoke. "Be quiet!" He said to the wind. He looked down at the water. "Be still!" He said.

Immediately the wind died down and the lake grew calm. The raging waves became just ripples and all was still. The disciples didn't know what to make of it.

"That was amazing! What sort of man is this?" they asked. "Even the wind and waves obey when He speaks to them."

The dazed but relieved disciples continued to the shore on the other side of the lake.

Jesus had calmed the storm on the lake and saved them. He had power over the storm because as God He has power over all creation.

Jesus saves us from the storms in our life, too, by saving us from sin, death, and the power of the devil.

The amazing picnic

There's a boy here with five barley loaves and two fish," said Andrew, "but that will never be enough to feed this crowd!"

The sun was beginning to set at the end of a long day. Jesus had taken His disciples away to find a bit of peace and quiet. He had heard how Herod had ordered the death of John the Baptist, His cousin, and He needed some time to grieve for a while.

The people had other ideas though. Someone had heard where Jesus was going, across the lake, and had spread the word. A great crowd, around 5,000, had taken to the roads and cut across the fields.

When Jesus landed on the shore, He found them all waiting for Him!

"Don't make a fuss," Jesus said to His disciples. "These people are like sheep without a shepherd. I'll talk to them."

That afternoon, Jesus taught the people about God's kingdom and He healed many who were sick. Now, it was evening.

"They'll all be getting hungry," said one of the disciples. As he said that, he was thinking, *So am I.*

"We don't have enough money to buy food for everyone," said another.

"Why not give them something yourself?" said Jesus. He didn't mean

to sound rude because He knew what He was going to do. It was then that Andrew brought the boy, with his food, to Jesus.

"It's all I have," said the boy. "I give it to You, though, if it will help."

Jesus instructed the disciples to organize the crowd and sit them down in groups on the grass. After this had been done, Jesus took the small basket and blessed the loaves and fishes, thanking God for them. Next, He broke up the bread and the fish and gave it to the disciples to hand out.

In and out of the crowd they went, breaking off pieces of bread and fish.

"Jolly good supper," said someone. "I wasn't expecting this."

Others in the crowd gobbled up the food too and it wasn't long until folk were sitting back and licking crumbs from their fingers.

Jesus told the disciples to clear away anything that was left over.

"Pick it all up and put the leftovers in a basket," He said.

To the amazement of the disciples, the crowd, and the young boy, there were 12 baskets of left-over food, yet everyone's hunger had been satisfied.

Jesus had fed the people, first with His Word and then wtih food. Jesus feeds us the same way, with His Word in the Bible and in the Lord's Supper.

Bartimaeus can see!

"I've never known it to be so busy. Why are all these people here?"

The question came from a man sitting by the side of the road. He could not see the crowd but his other senses were sharp. He could hear the sound of footsteps and knew there were hundreds of feet kicking up dust that he could taste in his throat. He could feel the crush and the heat of a great crowd milling around.

"Don't you know?" asked someone. "Jesus is passing through here on His way to Jerusalem. We're so pleased He has chosen to come to our city of Jericho. Everyone wants to see Him."

The man hung his head and his shoulders sagged.

"I want to see Him too," said Bartimaeus. How many

years had it been? He remembered barely the shapes and colors from his childhood. He could do no work and was reduced to begging on the streets. If no one helped him, he went hungry.

Bartimaeus gathered news by hearing bits of conversations. He had learned how Jesus had made an old woman well and how He had healed a paralyzed man. If He could do that for others, couldn't He help this poor, blind man too?

Bartimaeus sat up and turned this way and that trying to sense where Jesus was.

"Jesus, son of David," he cried, "have mercy on me!"

"Shush! Be quiet!" some of the crowd called. They didn't want anything to disturb Jesus. But the beggar called out again and the Man the crowd had all come to see stopped.

"Bring him here," said Jesus.

"Did you hear that, friend?" said someone nearby. "He's calling you." Some people in the crowd helped Bartimaeus up and led him across the road.

"What is it you want Me to do for you?" asked Jesus.

"Give me my sight again," pleaded the blind man. Jesus knew how much faith Bartimaeus had.

"You have your sight," Jesus said. "Your faith has made you well."

At that, Bartimaeus could see. What brightness! He blinked as the light flooded in.

"Oh, thank You, Master, thank You," cried Bartimaeus. The people joined in shouting about how wonderful it was that the beggar had his sight once more. Bartimaeus was so grateful he followed Jesus and the crowd along the road.

Just as Jesus restored sight to Bartimaeus, He restores life to all those who have eyes of faith.

The man with no friends

The tax collector had been trying to find a place to stand all morning. Now the sun was high in the sky and it was making him hot and bothered as he ran this way and that. He was desperate to see Jesus as He passed through the streets of Jericho. But Zacchaeus was too small and the crowd was too big!

"Hey! stop pushing," said a very large gentleman. Zacchaeus wasn't going to argue. He tried a bit further down the street.

"Excuse me, madam. Would you just move over a little? You are taking up rather a lot of space."

The lady turned around, looking furious.

Time to go, thought Zacchaeus.

Up ahead, Zacchaeus saw a large sycamore tree. He had the fine idea that if he could just climb it, he would have a grand view over everyone's head! He found a couple of hand-holds and pulled himself up. Reaching up, he took hold of another branch and climbed higher. Finally, he nestled on a branch and peered out between the leaves.

This was tremendous. So many people! The crowd following the carpenter from Nazareth was huge. How could Jesus take in all these faces? Then Zacchaeus felt those eyes turn toward him. Jesus put out His hand and beckoned.

"Come on down from there, Zacchaeus," Jesus called. "Yes, I can see you, come on. I could do with a drink and something to eat … at your house … now."

Zacchaeus struggled down from his hiding place.

"Oh, Jesus, You are most welcome to my home," he twittered. But some of the people grumbled.

"Why is He going to Zacchaeus's house?" someone asked. "He cheats us by collecting more tax than he should. He hands over the correct amount to the Romans but keeps the rest." People were pointing and the mood was turning ugly. But then, Zacchaeus had something to say.

"Jesus, please listen. I know I have often done wrong. I will give  half my belongings to the poor. Also, if I have cheated anyone, I will pay them back four times as much." Zacchaeus really did look ashamed.

Jesus spoke to him, but in a voice loud enough for everyone to hear.

"You have recognized your sin and are trying to put things right," said Jesus. "Well done, Zacchaeus. It is to save people like you that I have come."

Jesus came for all people, including sinners like Zacchaeus—including sinners like us.

The King on a donkey

"Hey! What do you think you're doing?" called the man. "Where are you going with my donkey and foal?"

He was quite reasonably a bit annoyed. Who were these two strangers untying his donkey and her young foal and about to lead them away? The two disciples of Jesus stopped. They looked at each other, seeming to know that this was going to happen. One of them spoke as he had been instructed by Jesus.

"The Master has need of them," he said simply.

The owner of the animals relaxed. He spoke more gently and the redness had gone from his face.

"Well, in that case, you may take them," he said.

Back outside the villages of Bethphage and Bethany, the disciples helped Jesus get on the donkey and He rode toward Jerusalem.

The word had already spread from Jericho that Jesus was on His way. The crowds had come out in huge numbers and were lining the streets. The noise was tremendous with people cheering and shouting. One young man called to his friends.

"Come, help me! I'm going to cut some palm branches," he shouted.

"Why are you doing that?" his friends asked.

"We'll lay them down on the road. It will be like rolling out the red carpet for the King!"

And so it was. Many others threw down their shawls and cloaks to pave the way.

"Hosanna!" they shouted.

"Blessed is He that comes in the name of the Lord. Hosanna in the highest!"

Some Roman soldiers looked on as the procession turned the corner and continued through the city gate. They had seen parades similar to this in Rome but never out here in the provinces.

Some of the people inside the city weren't sure what was going on.

"What's all the fuss about? Who is all the cheering for?" someone asked.

"It's Jesus from Nazareth!"

Jesus came to Jerusalem as the heavenly King. He comes today in Baptism and the Lord's Supper, and in the Bible, His holy Word.

A cruel death

They were all too busy. No one heard him as he stood facing Jesus, who hung there on the cross.

The Roman centurion had seen everything as events had unfolded; he seemed to have been on duty all week. He had been there, watching through the temple doorway, as Jesus had overturned the tables and sent the traders and moneychangers on their way.

"My Father's house is a house of prayer," Jesus had declared.

Later that week, the centurion had been a member of the guard sent to arrest Jesus in the Garden of Gethsemane. He could remember what one of Jesus' followers had said as he was about to betray Him to them.

"The man you are to arrest will be difficult to see in the torchlight," Judas had explained. "You'll recognize Him when I kiss Him on the cheek."

After taking Jesus to the Jewish High Priest, there was the back and forth between Pilate, the Roman governor, and Herod, the Jewish king. Neither wanted responsibility for this man.

Finally, Pilate had had enough. He stood in front of the crowd and offered them Jesus, the Teacher and Healer, or Barabbas, a murderer. When the crowd chose to release Barabbas and crucify Jesus, Pilate had asked for a bowl of water.

"I find this man has done nothing wrong,"

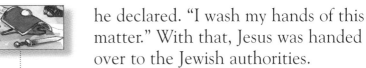

he declared. "I wash my hands of this matter." With that, Jesus was handed over to the Jewish authorities.

The other guards had made fun of Jesus. They'd stripped off His outer coat, dressed Him in a purple robe and made a crown out of twisted thorn twigs and pushed it onto Jesus' head. Then they spat at Him and punched Him.

Now Jesus was dying, nailed to the cross on the hill called Golgotha, "The Skull."

While some of the guards gambled to see who was going to have Jesus' robe, Mary, His mother, was in tears. The disciples were trying to console and comfort her as they watched in grief and shock. Some of the crowd jeered and shouted insults at Jesus.

"You saved others, why don't You save Yourself now?" they cried.

But the centurion gazed up at the face of Jesus. All week he had seen and heard what Jesus had done and said. "Truly, this man is the Son of God," whispered the centurion.

And He was. Jesus had come to earth and had taught, healed, and forgiven the people. As was God's plan, Jesus had come to save all people.

The first Easter Day

"Guards!" roared Pilate. "This person has my permission to remove the body of the man called Jesus. Let him through."

Joseph, from Arimathea, had recently cut a new tomb out of the rock. He had made a present of the tomb out of respect for the Master he followed.

He wrapped Jesus' body

in clean linen and laid it in the stone tomb. Then he strained to roll a large stone across the entrance.

The next day, the chief priests and Pharisees went to see Pilate.

"You will remember how Jesus said He would rise on the third day," they said. "We think His followers plan to steal the body and claim this has happened. This could cause more trouble than when He was alive."

Pilate didn't want that! "You may have a guard," he agreed.

So guards were stationed at the tomb and they sealed the stone.

The Sabbath day passed and the third day dawned.

"That felt like an earthquake!" cried one of the guards. They were so frightened they couldn't move.

Mary Magdalene and another woman, also named Mary, went to the tomb to prepare the body according to

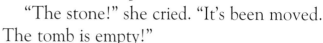

Jewish custom. When they arrived there, they gasped. Then Mary Magdalene ran to find Simon Peter and another disciple.

"The stone!" she cried. "It's been moved. The tomb is empty!"

The two disciples ran to the garden and found the grave clothes lying neatly folded inside the otherwise empty tomb. They were confused and wandered home. But Mary stayed in the garden, crying to herself.

"Why are you weeping?" The question came from one of two angels now sitting inside the tomb.

"I don't know where they have taken Jesus," she sniffed.

Whether it was the sun dazzling her or the tears in her eyes, she didn't recognize the man standing nearby. Thinking He must be the gardener, she asked if He had taken away Jesus' body.

"Mary," He said, simply. Instantly she recognized Jesus' voice.

"Teacher!" she exclaimed.

"Go and tell the others," He instructed her. And Mary, overjoyed that Jesus was alive, hurried to tell the disciples everything she had seen that morning.

Just as He had said, Jesus rose from the grave after three days. He had suffered and died for the sins of the world—our sins—and He had conquered death. Because Jesus makes us His own in Baptism, we have eternal life too.

Breakfast by the lake

"Well, who is it then?" asked one of the fishermen.

They strained their eyes toward the figure standing on the shore but, with the sun barely creeping over the horizon, they couldn't tell who was there. They heard His voice as it drifted over the calm water of the lake.

"Have you caught anything?"

"Huh! If only he knew," muttered one of them. Then he called out, "No! Nothing! Not even a minnow." He sounded very fed up.

"Cast your net on the other side of the boat. You'll find something then," said the stranger.

Some of the disciples were annoyed.

"Who does he think he is? We've been out all night and…"

"Let's give it a try," said one of the others. "We've nothing to lose."

So they dragged the net across the deck and cast out again. After a moment they started to haul the net back in.

But this time things were different.

"Come on, pull harder!"

"I'm pulling as hard as I can; it's too heavy!"

They had worked all night and not caught a thing. But this time they had caught so many fish their net nearly broke from the weight. John stopped and turned around. Suddenly, realization spread across his face.

"It's Him! It's Jesus," he gasped.

Without hesitation, Peter jumped from the boat and into the water. He waded ashore, leaving the others to bring in the marvelous catch.

When they all arrived, they could smell smoke. A small fire burned and breakfast was already cooking. There was some bread too.

"Bring some of the fish you've just caught," said Jesus. So they did.

"Come," said Jesus, "come here and have some breakfast."

He took some of the bread and passed it around and then He gave them some fish. It was a delicious breakfast and they were really pleased to see the Lord again.

Jesus told them it would not be long before He would leave them to be with His Father again.

But He used the time until then to appear to His disciples and others, teaching them and telling them what to expect.

In turn, the disciples went throughout the land, telling about Jesus and baptizing people in the name of the Father, the Son, and the Holy Spirit.

This edition published by Concordia Publishing House
3558 S. Jefferson Ave.
St. Louis, MO 63118-3968
ISBN 0-7586-0719-9

Published in the UK by CWR

First edition 2004

Copyright © 2004 AD Publishing Services Ltd
1 Churchgates, The Wilderness, Berkhamsted, Herts HP4 2UB
Text copyright © 2004 Christopher Doyle
Illustrations copyright © 1998 Roger Fereday

Editorial Director Annette Reynolds
Art Director Gerald Rogers
Pre-production Krystyna Hewitt
Production John Laister

Printed and bound in Singapore